How to Start a  500

Heikin Ashi Trader

SPLENDID ISLAND

Table of Contents

1. How to Become a Trader with only $500 at Your Stake? 3

2. How to Acquire Good Trading Habits? 10

3. How to Become a Disciplined Trader 19

4. The Fairy Tale of Compound Interest 27

5. How to Trade a $500 Account? 32

6. Social Trading 42

7. Talk to Your Broker 49

8. How to Become a Professional Trader? 57

9. Trading for a Hedge Fund 62

10. Learn to Network 64

11. Become a Professional Trader in 7 Steps 67

12. $500 is a Lot of Money 69

Glossary 71

More Books by Heikin Ashi Trader 75

About the Author 80

Imprint 81

1. How to Become a Trader with only $500 at Your Stake?

Most new traders, when starting out, have a small account. The sum may be different, but almost all of these traders start with the desire to increase this small capital sum quickly. This need is natural and understandable, but the urge to do so fast is the seed for future failure. Whether they start with $500 or $1000, most beginners feel that they are only a "small fish in the stock market." They want to change this as quickly as possible.

They believe that the only way to get to a big account is to multiply their little account fast. Because then, if the account is large enough, they can quit their job and make a living solely from trading. As such, they begin to look for trading strategies that promise them the highest possible returns. That these strategies usually are associated with high risks, they stubbornly ignore and plunge headlong into the adventure of trading.

The result is that most of these $500 accounts no longer exist after a maximum of 3 to 6 months. The statistics show that this is the likeliest outcome. If you start trading with the need to increase your account fast, you will give this goal all your energy and attention. This means that you will not focus your energy on what you are supposed to do first: to become a good trader, hence, to acquire good trading habits.

Even if you have access to more substantial funds, I would still advise you against transferring these funds to a trading account. You are at the beginning of your trading career and certainly not yet in a position to manage this capital effectively and responsibly.

First it is wise to learn to trade only a small account. If you only have about $500 or even less to trade, I see it as an advantage rather than a drawback. I understand the desire to make money fast all too well, as I had this need too when I started. This need led me to concentrate on multiplying this little capital fast, rather than, learn the craft.

Admittedly, $500 will not get you far. However, it is important that you learn to appreciate even this small sum and deal with it responsibly. As responsibly as you would if it were actually $500,000. Irresponsible is, of course, the use of disproportionate leverage that most brokers, unfortunately, make available. With $500 you can actually trade $50,000 with many forex brokers, but that does not mean that you should do it.

In my experience, most beginners overleverage themselves in the market. For example, I have traded more than $200,000 in capital with only $2000 in my account. This naturally means stress and a lot of adrenaline. While some individuals are specifically seeking these thrills, it is an unprofessional trading technique.

The result is that these "traders", hold far too long to loss positions, and hope that the market will graciously turn, so that they can at least approach breaking even. There is a well-known internet video of a trader who allowed his losing position to grow to $ -30,000. He could not believe that the market had not followed his analysis and merrily ran against his position. This recording was the apotheosis of a completely unprofessional approach. You will definitely not become a professional trader in this way.

In addition, most beginners have exaggerated ideas of how returns can be achieved in the market. Definitely, you can make 50% per month, even more. However, you will have to take high risks (i.e. overleveraging) to achieve this. Eventually, this leverage is going to work against you. This usually happens via a catastrophic trade, such as in the aforementioned video, which destroyed the entire account of the trader within few hours. I speak here from personal experience.

Please forget the idea of turning $500 to $50,000, or even to $5,000, within a short period. There exist many quieter and safer methods to grow your money. These work perfectly with $500 at the beginning. First, lower your return expectations. Instead, of 50% a month, I would act on the assumption of 20% annual return. If you can do that, you are good at it.

I know that I will probably disappoint some readers when I say making 1 to 2% a month are top performances. Nevertheless, they are actually top results, especially when you achieve this performance every month on a continuous basis.

Perhaps you are under the impression that you can earn $1000 a month with a $1000 account. I am sorry to disappoint you here, but such returns are possible only by incurring extreme risks. The chance that you will succeed at this, month after month tends towards zero. Get it out of your head! It will not work, and if this book can rid you of this illusion, my work is half-finished already.

I want to stress that there are alternatives to these exaggerated expectations. These alternatives are much more interesting and easier. You can realize your dream of a large trading account one day, but the path to it is probably different than you would imagine. Honestly, I wish I had someone said this to me at the beginning of my trading career. It would have spared me many years of futile attempts, trying to multiply a mini account using futures. Of course, you could collect experience in this way. However, these experiences I can pass on.

Who am I? I am a trader with over 15 years' experience in the markets, who has witnessed all the vicissitudes of the trading business. I have traded for a hedge fund in forex trading, as well as for managed accounts. I know this industry and its tricks, very well. I have repeatedly witnessed this little drama of a starting trader, driving his entire trading account on the wall, and I have done it myself several times. I know what it looks like and how it feels.

The problem is not the money. One can get over the loss of $500. You gained experience. It did not work out, but it is not a drama. There are also people who start with a $50,000 account, even with a $500,000 account, and these accounts often also no longer exist after 3 or 6 months.

Therefore, it is obvious that it is not the amount of capital at stake. It does not matter if you start with $500 or $50,000. Something seems to be going fundamentally wrong in this trading business, no matter how much money you have available. This desire to increase the starting capital quickly seems to lead to exactly the opposite. This applies for at least 95% of the beginners. I must confess, this is one of the saddest statistics I know.

Imagine if 95% of bakery apprentices would fail in the bakery, because baking little breads is too difficult a profession. That this is definitely not the case proves that people are doing something right in the bakeries. Baking bread is a profession that you can learn, provided you are willing to get up early and follow the instructions of the Master Baker.

I declare herewith, that trading and currency trading are no more difficult professions than baking. However, the prerequisite is that the new trader is willing to get up early (though not as early as the baker's apprentice) and follow the instructions of the "Master Baker".

Concerning trading, the first thing to take note of, is the instructions of the Master Baker. Unfortunately, this does not happen and that is probably the main reason the statistics are so disastrous, when it comes to success in trading. It is even worse. Not only are the instructions of the Master Baker not being followed, but also the "Master Baker" is simply not there. Most starting traders are just sitting alone in their room in front of the computer screen and romp through the market as they please.

This book is therefore about the instructions of the "Master Baker." It is up to you, dear reader, whether you take note or not. At least the "Master Baker" has done his duty.

2. How to Acquire Good Trading Habits?

It does not matter if you start your trading career with $500 or $50,000. I want to explain in this book why this is so. Trading is a profession, and must be learned like any other profession. You must first learn the "basics." As a baker, the best way to learn would be to make all your beginner's errors while you are still baking small rolls. The same can be said about trading: It is best that you make your rookie mistakes with the smallest possible account.

I know that a whole group of professional traders will get up and tell you that this does not make sense. I recommend it anyway. Of course, you can try out your strategies on a demo account (an account with play money). However, do not linger too long at this stage. Trading begins only when real money is involved, even if the amount is small.

I want to show you two paths that are open to you as a trader. Both have pros and cons (like everything else in life), but these are two real paths that will enable you, some day, to make a living by trading. These paths are also open those traders who have only a small sum, $500 or even less. Even if you cannot imagine now how you can ever enjoy a large trading account, have faith. You can do it.

The first way is by remaining a private trader. This means that you will build your trading business with your own money. How this is possible and what conditions must be met, I will explain in the first part of the book (chapter 2-6).

In the second part (7-11), I will suggest ways in which you can become a professional trader. A professional is a trader who trades with client funds and hereby earns his living. This is a different path than the first and requires, to a certain extent, a different preparation.

Nevertheless, both ways require one important thing: your effort in the first period will concentrate on acquiring good trading habits, rather than focusing on multiplying a small account quickly. Without good trading habits, you will never be a profitable trader. Neither a private trader who can live off his trading results, nor a professional who lives from the commission of his customers.

This is the groundwork of trading. Good trading habits are like the foundation of your future trading businesses. All your strength and concentration in the beginning should aim first at becoming a good trader. Consequently, the money will follow.

You should take this crucial (and more professional) point of view before you begin this profession. When you have wrong-headed views on this profession, your chances for success are low, hence, you are in for a long, rocky road, as was the case with me.

I myself naturally thought that I knew better and that an apprenticeship in the bakery was superfluous. I want to show the three most important good habits for a trader by a little experiment. That way, you know what you are getting into when you plan to take this profession.

First, I suggest you do 50 trades carried out with forex pairs, or, If you do not have a forex account, with equity indices.

These are the specifications:

1. Pick out any currency pair.

2. Throw a coin. If the coin displays head, then go long. If it shows you the number, then go short.

3. Immediately insert a trailing stop at 20 pips distance from the entry price.

4. If the position after 5 minutes is still in the loss, close it and move on to the next trade.

5. If the position after 5 minutes is in profit, do nothing. Let the trailing stop do the work.

6. You should only have three trades running simultaneously, in three different pairs.

7. Repeat this process until you have completed all 50 trades.

The attentive reader may recognize in this experiment that the three most important good habits of traders are hidden. I recommend that you carry out this experiment. You will be amazed at what results you can achieve, provided you adhere strictly to the rules.

Therefore, we have already arrived at habit number one. A good trader adheres to the rules without exception. Although it seems easy, more than 95% of traders do not do this.

The experiment may appear meaningless to some readers , since no attention is paid to the analysis of charts, that is, no time is wasted with the entry of trades. In addition, the reason a trade has been executed is completely ignored. Moreover, I even let chance decide, through the coin-toss, whether to go long or short, as if the entry is something completely unimportant.

There are, however, clear guidelines with respect to the exit rules. In other words, a trader who carries out this "experiment," is doing everything possible to minimize the losses. The 5-minute rule plays an especially important role here. Again, this is a good habit of successful traders.

If a trade does not work out after a short time or is not running in the right direction, there is no reason to stay in the trade. This may sound rigorous, and it is. Good traders are impatient with their losses and close them quickly, without hesitation.

This is a golden rule of the trading profession, namely, the preservation of capital is paramount. However, you will also perhaps protect an even more important capital: your trader's psyche.

Sticking to loser trades destroys, over time, your trader's psyche and leads, eventually, to something known as "Analysis Paralysis." One begins to look unnecessarily for "ideal" entries, although everyone knows that these do not exist.

Either you are at the right time at the right place in trading, or not. If not, then get out of the dust as soon as you can.

However, the trailing stop in this experiment does something different. It makes sure that you stay as long as possible in a position when the trade is running in the win. Again, this is a good trading habit: stay with your winners! If you can do that, you differ even from 95% of traders. Ideally, your trade should run until Friday afternoon. However, it is not likely, because the trailing stop will be reached eventually.

Nevertheless, this is an important exercise: Do not take too early gains as if you are in profit, but try to extract the maximum from the trade. This follows the two most important statements of the golden rule of trading: cut your losses, and let your profits run. 95% of traders do exacty the opposite.

I can well imagine that it will be difficult to close a trade that is only slightly in loss after 5 minutes Do it anyway. I also know what the objection is: "But the trade might go into positive territory in the next minute and then I might miss a profit!" Yes, that can happen, and it will happen repeatedly; it is part of the trader's existence.

The much higher probability, however, is that this trade is just not a winner but continues in the loss. That is why I recommend closing this position anyway and moving on to the next trade. When you learn that, you have acquired an important habit: No matter what happens, you do not tolerate losses anymore.

Regarding the entries, I do not want to be misunderstood. Of course, you can try through accurate chart analysis, to select your entries as accurately as possible. However, I would like to take this opportunity to express a clear warning from my experience: the importance of analysis is greatly overestimated. In my view, traders spend too much time with the analysis of charts. This is no different than trying to predict the future.

On the other hand, they spend too little time with the strict observance of their risk management, which is usually the root cause of their failure. I will hereby also not promote the trailing stop. This instrument certainly has advantages, but it also has disadvantages, of which I am aware. With trailing stops, trades are often stopped out too soon by random counter-movements, although the trend might be intact and there is no reason to get out of the trade.

The experiment is to let the trailing stop decide when the gains have been realized. In some cases, this will certainly be too early. However, this tool will allow you in some other cases to hold the position for a long time. This is also a good habit. Thanks to this experiment, you will learn the most important good habits of a professional trader. You will learn to follow your rules, to close losses quickly and to stay as long as possible with your winners.

Believe me; you do not need much more. If you acquire these habits, you will belong one day to the 5% that succeed in the markets.

This experiment can be repeated at will. Because, as we all know, habits are one of the hardest things to change. Try to stop smoking, if you are a smoker. There are traders who have been lugging around bad habits for years, and then wonder why success does not occur. Among them are also so-called professionals. Do not think that all "professionals" maintain these good habits; Only the successful ones do. With this foundation, I now would like to show you two ways that you can become a disciplined trader, even if you currently have a low capital base.

3. How to Become a Disciplined Trader

Once it has become clear that the principles are the same for all traders, whether they have $500 or more than $500000, I would like to suggest ways in which you can make a living from trading without gambling with one´s life. As already mentioned, most beginners have a completely wrong-headed idea of what returns can be made on the stock exchange. Experienced and disciplined traders generate 20 to 30% profits per year. In good years, this may be 40 or 50% sometimes. This means that these traders are creating monthly returns of 2 to 3%.

These returns are achieved with a reasonable risk management. Drawdowns generally remain below 15%. If you trade, one day, an account of several hundred thousand dollars, you will, I hope, have appropriated such a risk profile.

Now we come to your $500 account. I hope that you have realized that you cannot earn your living from this sum. However, what you may well be able to do is, just like the professionals, make a nice annual return of 20 or 30% earn with drawdowns that remain below 15%. This way, you prove to yourself that you can trade. That is the best thing that can happen to you.

For an account of $500, only the forex market is a realistic option. Therefore, look for a forex broker who will charge no fees for transactions. Many professionals have been led to conclude that it is simply, mathematically, not possible to trade a $500 account, because the fees alone eat up the account. Not even to mention a reasonable risk management approach.

As an example, I want to mention a trade in EUR/USD with a mini lot ($10,000). This has been, until recently, the smallest possible unit that you could trade with most brokers. If you set your stop 50 pips away from the entry price, you risk 50 pips or $50. At $500, this is 10% of your trading capital! If you lose in this way 5 times in a row, which is not uncommon, you have lost already half of your capital. If you risk 10% of your capital per trade, you are not a trader. You are a kamikaze pilot.

The criticism of these mini accounts consists essentially of two arguments; First, you can only trade one strategy at a time. Therefore, you are completely dependent on the results of this one strategy. You cannot diversify. Second, you cannot have a reasonable risk management, having just this small sum to your name, as this example in EUR/USD clearly shows.

It is fortunate that some brokers had this insight, and they are offering currently their customers microlots. These are only 1/10 of a minilot. Therefore, you are trading with only $1000.

In the same example, you would then risk only $5 or 1% of your capital. This sum is much closer to a reasonable risk management for private traders, although I personally still find 1% risk per trade too much.

It may not sound exciting to trade with $500 in a disciplined way for perhaps 12 months and consequently get a profit of 20%, or $100 more in your account. However, this is exactly what you should do. You should learn to trade this tiny account as if it were a million-dollar account. For this purpose, I recommend to keep a detailed trading journal that logs all trades exactly. In addition, it is useful to make weekly or monthly statistical evaluations.

How to do this exactly, I have outlined at length in my book, "How do I rate my trading results?" You can find the book on Amazon. The task, therefore, is to carry out a disciplined strategy in the market you have selected for at least one year. Mind that I said one strategy and not seven.

Many beginners start with one strategy. If then the first losses show up they are disappointed, discard the strategy and look for something new. Then the cycle starts again from the beginning. This behaviour definitely does not belong to a good trader's habits!

Therefore, you should stay consistent with your chosen strategy, no matter what happens. The reason is simple. If you have never traded with one strategy for a year, you will never learn this strategy in a profound way. Each strategy has loss phases. It does not matter which one you choose, as long as it is profitable.

This alone will discipline you enormously. If you replace your strategy repeatedly, you never learn to know yourself as a trader. That is the point, so stay with your choice once made. In addition, you should keep a detailed trading diary. By that, I mean a full coverage of your trades. Such a journal should contain at least the following data:

- Date of Entry: i.e. the date when you have opened the position

- Name of the forex pair

- Entry price: the price you have bought (long) or sold (short)

- Stop Loss: the risk you have run into in this trade

- Take Profit: the target that you wanted to achieve with your trade

- Position Size: how many micro-lots you have bought

- Date of exit: i.e. the date when you have closed the position

- P/L (Profit/Loss) in pips: how many pips have you earned

You can still add other data, but these are definitely the most important.

Why should you do that? If you consistently collect this data from all your trades, you get a wealth of information about your trading, which is worth more than all the trading books together. You may find out that you are better in short selling than going long. If so, would it not be reasonable to specialize exclusively in short selling? Do you know that some traders are owned 100% short sellers, who never go long? They do this because they have recognized, based on their data, that to go short is the best thing for them. I, for example, am a good short seller and a bad long trader. You might notice that most of your losses are in a particular forex pair. I myself am bad in the GBP/USD. That is why I avoid this pair most of the time.

For that, I am good in Swiss francs, and good in the USD/CAD. I know that just thanks to my trading journal. Isn´t that valuable information?

At the end of the week (or month), you should evaluate your trading data. This, too, I have shown in detail in my book "Scalping is Fun! Part 3: How do I rate my trading results?".

Here are the key figures for your statistics:

- Number of trades per week / month / quarter

- Number of winners

- Number of losses

- Number of break-even trades

- Average win

- Average loss

- Hit rate (your number of winners in percent)

- Payoff Ratio (profitable or not and how profitable?)

- Expectancy (expectation of your system)

The statistical information that can be found in your trading journal is perhaps even more valuable than the trading data itself. They show how robust your system is. Moreover, such an evaluation also shows at which screws you need to turn eventually to make your system more profitable. Maybe your losses are a little too high and you should set the stop loss closer or farther away.

Maybe you always want to win (the hit rate), and you do not pay attention to the height of the profits. The trader whose career I describe in detail in my book on Money Management had this problem. Consistently maintaining a trading journal also belongs to the good trading habits. Make it so from the beginning of your career, even if you have only a $500 account.

4. The Fairy Tale of Compound Interest

Before we take the next step, we have to deal with something that haunts in many Internet forums: namely, the story of compound interest, also called "the greatest force on earth." It is almost too good to be true, and many traders actually believe that it is possible to let their tiny account grow to a large account within a short time thanks to the compound interest effect.

The compound interest effect goes something like this: let us say, for simplicity, that you have $1,000 trading capital. Your (not immodest) goal is to earn 10 pips per day in the currency market on average.

The statement goes like this: On day 1, you make 10 pips and therefore have $ 1,010 in the account. On the second day, you make 10 pips again. Now, you have $ 1020. After 20 days, you are already proud of having $ 1,220 in the account. This is, after all, 22% in your first month!

You eventually need 70 days to double your account. You will then have $2000 to the account, provided you have gained 10 pips a day on average and you raise nothing from your account.

Since the capital is "growing" every month, you can of course risk "somewhat" more every month. You increase your position size with the increasing balance. In the first month, you are still trading with a minilot ($10,000). Since after one month you have $1200 in the account, you increase your position to $12,000. After two months, you are trading with $17,000, and so on.

Perhaps you are still not impressed by these figures. The idea is that if you do this in the next few months consistently, you will eventually experience the power of compound interest. If you are trading in this disciplined manner, your trading account will stand after 12 months at $24,000. If you do it again in the second year, you can call $500,000 your own.

You must then "only" trade three months until you are dollar millionaire. Mind you, with 10 pips per day! Convenient, is it not? You can do the math in a quiet hour, but it is true. You can be a forex millionaire with "only" 10 pips per day within 3 years.

I know that many beginners are impressed by this compound interest story when they hear of this idea for the first time. You do not need to be a mathematical genius to understand this simple calculation. It is the secret hope of many trading beginners that they will be able to achieve this masterpiece, thanks to their trading skills. If you succeed, give me a call, you would probably be the first in the world.

Why does almost nobody put this into practice? Theoretically, the calculation is correct, and I certainly do not mean that the compound interest effect is not working. It works safely and, in principle, every trader is trading with some sort of compound interest effect.

You probably guessed what the issue is. In this calculation, there are some "unknowns," which have not been taken into account. These unknowns have, of course, what it takes. It has a lot to do with good or bad trading habits, of which we have already spoken.

If you initially worked hard on your good trading habits, the opportunity certainly exists that you will experience some form of compound interest effect. However, say goodbye to the illusion that you could trade and make an average of 10 pips per day, or, if you want, 50 pips per week, as desirable as this might be.

The reality looks more like this: In some weeks, you will make perhaps 36 or 128 pips. However, it could be that the week after you have a 92 pips loss. In addition, the next week you do not trade, because you must stay in bed with influenza.

You will experience good days or weeks, where you will achieve good results and you will experience poor, even bad weeks.

The progress?

A trader who is working on their weaknesses (and on their strengths) will surely make progress. Nevertheless, these do not come immediately. Sometimes you have the feeling that nothing happens for a long time, and then suddenly there is a breakthrough and you are trading much better than before. Many traders need to experience the destruction of their first, and often their second, 500-dollar account. You need not be ashamed of it. Several times, I myself have brought smaller accounts to

$0. This was, of course, because of a lack of discipline.

After such a debacle, it is often good to take a break and think about your trading strategy. You would not believe how much better you can trade after such a break!

With increasing confidence, you might succeed in significantly increasing a small account. You should experience at least a doubling before ever transferring additional money to the trading account. Remember what we said in the first part on good trading habits.

5. How to Trade a $500 Account?

You will start to trade this little account with extreme caution. Of course, it depends on your strategy, if you risk 50, 20, or 10 pips per trade. The exercise consists mainly of preserving the capital. If you do, then you have already taken the first important step to success. Of course, your account will grow much more slowly in this way. However, do not forget: Your goal should not be to increase your $500 as soon as possible.

For the time being, you should use this sum to learn to trade. This means, in the first place, to achieve a regular return with a manageable risk. Returns of 2 to 3% a month there are already outstanding, especially when the risk (drawdown) remains below 10%. Find out more in the chapter on professional trading.

The idea to grow a mini account of $500 by virtue of compound interest to $1,000,000 or even $100,000 is a total crazy idea. It is unlikely that you will succeed, and this goal will overwhelm you immeasurably. You will again take too big of risks in order to achieve this. Do you see the pattern?

First, it is about learning your craft. If possible, try not to think on the money. As I said, 2 to 3% per month is already good. Consider this: 2% on a $ 500 account is $ 10. Let us be honest. Working, disciplined, for a whole month for $10? This will not bring you forward financially. I hope you understand the absurdity of this idea. Just say goodbye to this idea to earn money from this little capital.

Is it not, then, completely pointless to trade a $500 account?

No, it is not. Learn your craft with this small sum. If you are able to proliferate this account in the course of some time without taking great risks, you have yourself proved that you can trade. Trading is a craft and a profession that needs time to be learned. Half a year is a short time. As a rule, the learning curve of most traders, I know, will take much longer.

One consideration is thus the above described: simply not to try to make money with a $500 account. This trial period then only serves to learn the craft.

There is a second approach that makes sense, as well. Some traders with a small account have the goal to earn an average of $10 a day. This is a manageable goal, is it not?

You may say, "$10 a day? Are you joking? That's pure child's play!" Maybe. However, can you make this $10 without risking more than $10, and every day? It is a money target, not necessarily 10 pips. So, do not start and say, "I need to earn $200 a day, so that I can get $4000 from my trading account in the month."

It mostly turns out that that $4000 is usually the exact sum that people need per month in order to pay their bills. In other words, they need this money. Therefore, they have to be successful in order to achieve this goal. Can you see this? They do something not out of joy or because they want to learn something. They do it because they have to.

Moreover, if it does not succeed, it brings them serious troubles.

By this, they put themselves under unnecessary pressure. The consequences are often overtrading, taking too many risks, or trading with too high a leverage. I think you suspect already know what will happen next. Someone who is under pressure will fail eventually. That is exactly what happens when you hear of a spectacular loss in the stock market. I myself have fallen several times into this trap, and I can tell you, those were not my most glorious days.

The traders, on the other hand, who want to trade for only $10 on average per day, have probably set themselves a realizable goal. They also are not under the pressure to earn their living from it. $10 per day in a stock index or in a Forex pair is feasible. This trader would achieve his or her goal regularly. Thus, they condition themselves for success. Success is then something that feels light, and no extraordinary efforts are required.

$10 per day as a daily goal is, at 20 trading days, $200 per month. That might not sound like a significant sum of money, but do you know how much money you (with the low interest rates of today) must have in your bank account today to be paid interest returns of $200? Let us take a simple money market account with a maturity of 3 months. You would need about $1 million!

Therefore, if you could "earn" $10 on the stock market on a daily basis, this would be as if you had 1 million in your account. You can see that this goal is not modest.

Believe that a trader who can boast this "success" will find, after a while, ways and means to trade larger sums with the same ease. He or she will do it.

Granted, with an additional $200 a month you will not change your financial situation significantly. However, it is vital to make profits at all. You would not believe how great you can feel as a trader, if you have completed a positive month. You have the feeling that you have achieved something, which is the case. This is important to emphasize, because for people who are not active on the stock exchange, $200 is of course a ridiculous sum. They would not get up in the morning for that. For you, it is the proof that you have completed your apprenticeship in the bakery of trading successfully. You have acquired good trading habits, and that is precisely what matters.

There is another reason why I am not a big fan of a strict compounding effect: Reward yourself from time to time. Cunning traders do this. If you have, for example, traded disciplined and made a nice profit for the week, get a part of that gain from your account and make something great with it. Perhaps an evening in the movies with your beloved? The important thing is that it feels like a reward. It signals to your subconscious, "Well, done! Continue in this way!" It is worth it.

Nobody leaves all the money available on the brokerage account from $500 up to 1 million. It is not necessary and just a completely crazy idea. The compound interest effect occurs at some point, but often different than you would expect it. Every trader is different and is differently capitalized from there and has different resources (not only money but also time). Sometimes you will have the feeling that it can go fast, but you might also experience periods when your strategy is not working so well.

Many traders simply want to take a few months' break after a losing streak. Some come only back after a year with fresh ideas. They have perhaps attended some seminars or simply read a good book that will give them a completely new perspective on the stock exchange. Thus, they start with renewed vigour.

So, you see: The learning curve is not as smooth as one might think. There are fractures, breaks, and interruptions. The success itself also is not linear. There are times where you get the feeling you will never learn it, and then there is suddenly a breakthrough. A small change in your trading habits or a tip from an experienced professional may cause this. It comes in waves, and waves run back occasionally. If you then are able to generate regular returns, only then you should think about to trade with larger sums. From here, there are two possibilities.

You can decide to become a professional trader and to trade with client money. How to do this, I will tell you in Chapter 8. Alternatively, you may decide to stay a privateer, trading perhaps only part-time and still working at your day job. Whatever you decide, try to operate your trading as a business. Even if your business still yields little money and you are trading with a very small sum, try to trade as if you had a capital of $1 million. This profession depends strongly on the inner attitude. The more seriously you do this, the sooner a door will open to you that offers you the chance to realize your dreams.

If you have taken seriously the path to become a good trader first, you will experience that things will happen that you do not hold possible now. There might people coming to you, offering you money to trade for. Whether you should accept this money is another matter. You should decide only after careful consideration. It has much to do with the seriousness of which I spoke earlier. As long as you are not a disciplined trader who knows the craft, under no circumstances should you manage money from other people. I hope this speaks for itself.

It even can happen to you that a hedge fund calls you. That happened to me once. This fund was in trouble and urgently looking for a trader who was able to generate at least a little positive return for their customers. Nothing else was working. I started to trade and soon made gains for the fund. Nevertheless, the management had apparently not learned its lesson. All the problems had arisen because the automatic trading systems, which the Fund had initially used, only burned money.

Therefore, I came in the morning and began to trade the account successfully, but the management was apparently so convinced of their automated trading systems that they ran these again at night. The result was that the gains that I had earned during the day were destroyed at night by the robots. Can you imagine a more absurd situation? Believe me: Even with the so-called professionals, it sometimes goes haywire. Talents are always in demand. Now do you understand why you should first learn to trade in a disciplined way? These people also know that you do not have $5 million available to trade. If this were the case, you would probably not be interested in the job.

It may be of course happen that you suddenly come into money or even still had some money saved up that you had not previously used for your trading. When you are ready and have the feeling that you can deal in a responsible way with this amount, you can dare.

Do me a favour, however: Do not put the whole sum in your trading account. You will probably do it anyway, but I have said it at least.

This is the most common case. Most traders I know are trading with their own money and that's a good thing. Managing money from other people increases the stress considerably. Can you cope with this and achieve good performance anyway?

Maybe you inherit a sum of money one day. This, too, is of course possible. Should you accept money from relatives? Frankly, I would advise you not to. If someone gives you money and says, "I do not care if you burn it or grow it," then you might think about whether you accept this money. In my experience, most relatives do not say that sentence. Most look rather with a critical eye at your "new activity" as a trader, or give you the money with expectations. I would be careful, because no one knows if you will be able to meet these expectations.

6. Social Trading

A good alternative for undercapitalized traders is Social Trading. I have experienced this myself and can only recommend it to a very ambitious trader. Some of these sites are now working very professionally, and much more transparent than any investment fund or asset management. Here, in recent years, a small revolution has arisen in the area of money management and I hope that this "democratization" of asset management may continue to develop so that many people on this planet can benefit from it.

It is precisely here that the good habits and disciplined trading are in high demand. All your trades and their statistical evaluation are totally transparent and open cost for the entire world. Can you imagine this: you trade and the whole world is watching? Nevertheless, this is happening with Social Trading.

Social Trading platforms are not more than websites that bring together traders and potential investors. Investors have the money and the traders have (hopefully) the ability to multiply that money. There are of course rankings and the investor can choose his traders. He selects perhaps because of their trading style. Better, he chooses due to the disciplined trading behaviour, how the trader earns the yield, and the low level of risk. At least, the smart investors do this.

In addition, professional asset managers look now at Social Trading and consider whether they will invest a portion of their customer deposits there. Is that not incredible? It is definitely a fantastic opportunity for an ambitious trader! Now, do you understand why you should first learn to trade responsibly and disciplined with your $500 account? If you can do this, you can start with a clear conscience at one of the Social Trading platforms.

It will provide you with an account with "fictitious money," which you can trade. If your results are good, and you have built a good track record (after a few months), you may soon get your first customers and therefore earn money. The earning models differ; so have a clear look at it, because this will ultimately determine how much money you can earn with your trading.

Now, we want to look at the compensation model of a social trading platform more in detail. It usually works with one or more brokers. These brokers are most likely called Introducing Broker. That is, this broker connect between its clients and a so-called prime broker. A prime broker is the place where the settlement of securities transactions actually take place. These are generally well-known institutions such as JP Morgan, Credit Suisse, Deutsche Bank, etc.

Most introducing brokers in the retail business therefore have a connection to a prime broker. Those are not interested in small accounts. The Introducing Broker performs this task. These houses are familiar to most retail investors. Now, we look at the entire food chain of a Social Trading platform:

1. Prime Broker

2. Introducing Broker

3. Investment Management

4. Social Trading Platform

5. The Trader

You see, many people eat from this cake if the trader performs a transaction. That is also the reason why the spreads in Social Trading generally are higher than if you simply open an account with an Introducing Broker. Expect 2 to 3 pips spread on the EUR/USD, thus twice or even three times more than usual. That is also the reason why pure scalping in Social Trading is not working. The conditions just are not there to do this. Too many people earn on the spread.

However, if you have developed a Day trading- or a swing trading strategy that generates good return, you will also earn money with this model. Depending on the model, you will mostly be paid per-generated standard lot. As a beginner, you might initially get $1, once you generate one standard Lot (100,000 $) transaction volume. This may not sound like much, but if you do this 20 times a day, this can become a decent income.

If, by good trading, you manage to climb on the higher levels, you can earn up to $5 per lot. When you arrive here, in general, you will make a good living of your trading. This will of course only be successful if you actually can offer an added value (a good return) to your customers and if you do not senseless trades to generate as much as possible on commissions.

Therefore, have a talk with the management of the Social Trading Platform. They will be able to help due to their experience how you can balance out best the number of trades with the best earning potential for you. Commissions are therefore an excellent way to earn your living as a trader. If there is still at the end of a profit participation, the better. However, you must first be able to be able to pay your bills and to meet your expenses. This is especially true when things are not going as well with your trading, or if you get involved in a drawdown (a period in which you lose more than you gain).

If you trade only your own money, you will earn just nothing in this period, which may well lead to stress. However, if you are connected to a social trading platform, you will still earn more on the transactions that you perform. If you have previously satisfied customers, they will not run straight away if things do not work out as well for a while, if the drawdown is kept within limits. Therefore, if you become a social Trader "first," you can focus on your job as a trader and do not need to take care of the customers. That will change, if you should one day decide to trade for a professional asset management.

Some Social Traders earn five-digit monthly sums. For them, the dream of a successful trading career has already been fulfilled. Prerequisite is, as always, a positive return with manageable (predictable) risks. Each platform here offers the necessary tools to calculate your risk management. You can therefore determine your risk profile before you begin to build up a track record. I strongly recommend thinking about it for a while.

Traders who generate 20 to 30% on an annual basis with a maximum drawdown of 10 to 15% may have a better chance than traders who achieve the 70% return, but take risks of 45%. The reason is simple: usually small investors are attracted by the high returns. The retail investor thinks high return = rapid capital appreciation. If you put on the mass of the little ones, I can assure you that your "customers" are faster gone than you can think if you experience a loss series.

In contrast, the professional always looks only at the risk. His concern is, "How much loss can be expected at a maximum when I entrust my client funds to this trader? Logical or not?" The consequence is that the trader with the restrictive risk management will receive the larger accounts. Larger accounts mean more capital to trade. More capital means a greater share of the commissions for you as a trader.

7. Talk to Your Broker

If you for any reason do not like Social Trading, of course there are plenty of other ways to get to client funds. One of the most direct ways is to talk to your broker. This person or group of people has contacts with many people with money. It is the job of a broker to find these people. If you want to manage customers' money with your trading system or strategy, you might consider having a conversation with your broker.

Even if your broker should be dedicated only to retail customers (private customers), it can be worthwhile to talk with him. You never know whom he knows. If you are an active customer with him, he will always have an open ear for what you have to say. It is best to make an appointment with him. Better yet, invite him to dinner. You will be amazed what people entrust to you if you do them a favour.

There is another reason why you should talk with your broker before you start trading. If you plan one day to trade client funds, you must also be able to demonstrate that you can do that. That means that you need to present a track record that is authenticated in some way. This is also called "building credibility." Without credibility, it might become difficult ever to be admitted to an interview.

A certification can, of course, be done in different ways. You can go to a notary or you can even let perform an audit by one of the well-known accounting firms like KPMG or Deloitte. However, I doubt if you will get this done with your $500 account. Not to mention the horrendous fees for such an audit.

It is much easier to ask your broker, who is tracking your trades anyway, to authenticate your results in some way. This certification is not hard proof, as from a notary or an auditor, but at least you have something in your hand that was reviewed by a third party. Now you can safely approach an asset management with this document, although further tests might be coming at you.

Another possibility to reach an authentication if you track your trades via the platform myfxbook.com. This platform is now very well known and many traders have built up here a remarkable record of accomplishment. Do not underestimate an excellent record in a social trading platform. This may well be considered proof that you can trade. Social trading is a great way for traders to distinguish themselves.

Many brokers have an in-house asset management themselves. It is part of their business, even if only a small part. You will find this mostly under the term "managed accounts." Moreover, you will be amazed how mediocre these professional asset managers often are. So, do not let yourself be intimidated by the words "professional" or "asset management." Behind those words, you will too often find a trader who has the same troubles and problems as you. Often some broker even let their managed accounts simply run on, even though they know that they are not very good.

Why, you might ask? As long as at least one customer participates in this program, this "asset manager" will incur fees or commissions. Because of this, the broker always makes money no matter how successful he runs his "asset management."

Who knows, maybe you are the one who will breathe new life into this branch of your broker. If you offer him an interesting strategy, which differs from the known, your broker will certainly look at. It is also not difficult. After all, you are his customer. He has a complete insight into your trading history. He knows exactly whether what you do has hand and foot or not. Expect that also here the remuneration models can be very different. Just as, in Social Trading the broker will probably offer you a share of the commissions or the spread.

What percentage you will receive as a trader depends on your negotiating skills. Everything is possible here up to 50%. However, please remember that you are the one who is doing the work and creating added value. Do not sell yourself too cheaply.

If your broker does not offer managed accounts, you should not stop looking for one. A simple Google search will do it. Enter the term "managed accounts" and you can chose several asset managers from the list. Some of them will be other brokers that you may not know about. Others might be pure asset managers without brokerage. These houses (and their websites) can look very secretive and discreet. That should not deter you from calling them up and asking about the conditions for traders anyway. The worst thing that can happen to you is that they tell you politely that they have no need at the moment.

However, you should not have the expectation that you will be welcomed with open arms. These jobs are in high demand and there is a lot of competition. Again, the same rules apply as elsewhere. Only disciplined traders with good habits have a chance here to take action. If there is a "social proof" for your skills in Social Trading, you can assume that professionals screen you at an asset management firm. Here will be the proof of whether or not you have acquired good habits at the beginning with your $500 account and if you have mastered your craft. Although this is already excellent, and by this you stand out from 95% of all traders out there, it is usually not sufficient to act as a trader at an asset management.

Asset management do not have only one trader who manages client funds but usually several. In recent years, of course, more automated trading systems that do not need to pay the rent and do not need health insurance have taken over their jobs. If an asset manager has the choice between an excellent trading system and a mediocre trader, the choice is unlikely to be very difficult.

In plain language, this means that you have to offer something special to the house. Preferably, something they do not have yet. Suppose you have developed a dignified day trading system on the EUR/USD based on support and resistance, which achieves good results with low drawdowns. However, the asset management has already two traders who trade the Forex market and perhaps even an automatic forex breakout system. What would be the added value to this company?

So, try to offer something that surprises. Is there a trading niche in which only you have an expertise? It may not always be Forex or futures. Perhaps you are a specialist in Mongolian stocks. The Mongolian stocks lead to a further criterion that is important and that you should understand before you approach an asset management.

I do not know exactly how many Mongolian stocks there are and how much the Mongolian stock exchange is capitalized. It's great, if you can trade these stocks successfully with your $500 account by buying 50 stocks each time. But can you also carry out your strategy if you have to order 50,000 stocks in Oulang Bator without too much slippage (slippage: the trader gets a slightly worse price, because the order book is not liquid enough)?

You must be able to answer this question very clearly. So, the real question is, "Is your business scalable?" Only then, the asset management will be interested. Finally, they must sell the product "trading Mongolian stocks" to potential customers.

You see, it's not that simple. Your product should be feasible not only in large numbers; it should also be understandable for an interested customer, what you are doing. If the customer first has to learn Mongolian... you get what I mean.

Here, of course, shows up again the advantage of the Social Trading incidentally. When Social Trading you are anonymous and you do not know your customers. They also have no contact with you. It is not desirable and it is usually better, you concentrate completely on your trading.

But if you switch on the institutional side and offer managed accounts, it can happen to you, you will have to explain a client who wants to invest $250,000 where Mongolia is situated on the map and why this is such an interesting market. That this may not be an easy conversation is hopefully clear to you.

8. How to Become a Professional Trader?

The decision to become a professional trader might perhaps not come overnight, and is possibly growing with your increasing skills and confidence. However, do not think that you must have oversized skills or that you must achieve even phenomenal returns to be "worthy." In the world of asset management and hedge funds, completely different laws prevail than in the world of private investors. It is therefore good if you are reasonably prepared for what awaits you there.

There are many ways you can become a professional trader. Believe me, chance and a bit of luck play safely here. Nevertheless, even this career can be planned and carried out successfully like any other. One thing you should know from the outset. If you are going to trade larger accounts with client money, say goodbye to the idea to do this with scalping. Scalping works well on smaller accounts or if you stay privateer. Then, you can choose your broker.

Once you go to a professional asset management, you cannot choose your broker. So, you will experience conditions that you may not always like. It also does not help you to complain if you get a spread of two pips on EUR/USD, or if you are regularly confronted with partial executions and slippage. You generally cannot change this. Therefore, prepare yourself to trade a strategy that works on higher periods (hourly chart, four-hour chart or daily chart). A $1 million account is not the same as a $500 account.

In any event, it is always a good idea to build a strong track record. This of course has to happen on a life account. Try to trade in a disciplined matter for at least one year. Try to keep a conservative risk management. This means that you do everything possible to ensure your maximum drawdown remains below 10%. If possible, even less than 5%. If you can generate an annual return of 12-15% with a drawdown of less than 5%, chances are that professionals will have a serious look at your trading record. A concise trading journal, with detailed statistical analysis, is essential. If you cannot say at the interview what your payoff ratio is, you will have a problem.

The reason is very simple. An asset manager, essentially, does nothing more than selling financial products. One of these financial products might be you one day, with your robust trading system. Of course, customers are greedy and want the highest possible return for their money. However, if you calmly ask the customer how much risk he would be willing to take in order to achieve this high rate of return, he becomes a little more subdued. Excessive fluctuations in the account he does not like either, of course.

That is why asset managers are interested in systems and traders who can meet those needs. It is therefore much more important to have a quiet capital curve. Traders who produce a "boring" return of 12% per year with no significant variations on their equity curve have a much better chance to get a job than the many highfliers who make 100% per year. The traders who manage to be successful over a long period are not, per se, those with the highest returns. Successful professionals work with almost no leverage.

The mind-set of a professional is thus different from that of a private investor. Private investors want the highest possible return. The professional is looking especially at how this return is achieved. If it has been bought with high risks, he will probably not be interested in your product.

Do not forget: The professional has to sell this strategy! If the volatility of the capital curve is low and the trader has the drawdowns under control, then such a product can easily be sold to an affluent client. Incidentally, you always can leverage such a conservative product also. Then, 12% yearly becomes 24 %, or even 36%.

If you have your record, certified by your broker, do not expect to get a $1 million account immediately. Depending on the asset manager, you could even be asked to first open yourself an account at the house broker and trade this for 3 months with your strategy. If done successfully, you might sit together with the management for a second interview. If you have done well by then, they may offer you an account of $25,000 or $50,000 to trade.

I hope you realize that you still will not be able to earn your living out of this capital, since it might take at least the tenfold of this amount to do so. However, that may come faster than you expect, if the management is satisfied with your performance.

If you have gotten far enough to trade a $300,000 account in a disciplined way, then you are already very close to achieving your dream. Each asset management firm has its own idea of how a new trader has to be build up. Also, do not forget the psychological pressure that comes to you. It is another matter if you buy five standard lots in a currency pair than if you buy only five minilots. Even this "hurdle" you will have to take one day, if you want to become a professional.

9. Trading for a Hedge Fund

As regards hedge funds, I will be brief. It is possible to obtain a job at a hedge fund, but it is increasingly difficult. The largest trading books are now managed primarily by machines. Hedge funds have become "fussy" hence. They will surely not give a job to a "nobody" who does not provide an exceptional performance. The hardest entrance is for traders who specialize in currency trading. This process is now largely automated.

In addition, the regulators also intervene in this play. After the recent scandals around the manipulation of exchange rates, in which several large commercial banks were involved, the authorities want to see the "discretionary" trading restricted. Even if you achieve top performance in forex and you can demonstrate an outstanding record, you probably will find it difficult to land here. It is not impossible, but the odds are not good.

Add to that the fact that you will hardly get a job without a university degree. Hedge funds prefer to give jobs to graduates with an MBA or another

Masters. In addition, more and more traders compete with a PhD in statistics or mathematics as financial mathematics in the industry become ever more important. Can you compete with these people?

10. Learn to Network

It will now become clear that it is not enough, as so often in life, that you have mastered your craft. It often comes down to who you know, if you want at least to have the chance to be summoned for an interview. I can say from personal experience that, in this industry, most doors have opened for me because I knew this or that person. Either I had a conversation with them at one of the many financial fairs that exist, or I sat down with a small group after a lecture and got to know certain people in this way.

If you have to tell something interesting to a trader or a finance professional, you will always find an open ear. This alone certainly doesn't result in a job, but the one or the other interesting contact can help you get there. Although the whole trading industry is increasingly technical and computerized, it is nevertheless still carried out by people. People want attention, they want to be understood and valued by others. Do not forget that.

Also online, you can, of course, start networking, although to my experience this is far less effective than to contact somebody directly. Nevertheless, the online networking complements the personal contacts and it ensures that the people who might one day may be interested in you are able to keep an eye on you. It is also not a bad idea to post an interesting content contribution from time to time. This may be an interesting analysis of a stock or a currency pair. It may also be an original view of the current monetary policy of a central bank. It is not required, but it helps to increase your credibility in the industry.

From now on, you should no longer go to Facebook when you want to "out" yourself. If you want to get a foot into the financial sector, you need a profile with the business network LinkedIn. This network is the largest and you will usually find there all the people who you met at trade shows or presentations again. Even your broker is represented here, as well as many hedge fund managers and asset managers. So, get out and keep in touch with those individuals.

It is certainly not wrong even to call up some of these people, even if you might not be looking for a job. The more qualified leads you have, the better. You never know from which corner your next career step will come.

11. Become a Professional Trader in 7 Steps

1. Learn to trade and start right at the beginning with good trading habits. Visit seminars or workshops. Read good trading books. Gain experience.

2. Work out a strategy that suits you. It may be something simple, just no scalping.

3. Pick out a broker who is willing to authenticate your trade record. If your current broker refuses this or gives you only a vague response, keep looking for another broker.

4. Trade for 1 year with your strategy without change. Have a conservative risk management. Try to keep the maximum drawdown less than 10%. You can day trade, but work with stops that are farther away. Trade in a way so that you could carry out this strategy easily even with $10 million.

5. Start networking immediately. Make contacts in the industry. Go to trade shows. Talk to fund managers and asset managers. Ask what conditions new traders need to bring to trade for their house.

6. Approach a variety of asset management firms with the aim to trade customer funds. Start small and work your way up.

7. Keep in touch with other asset managers or funds. Even if you have a job now, you do not know if you will still have it next year. Keep moving.

12. $500 is a Lot of Money

Even if you cannot even imagine this perhaps today, you can become a trader with a $500 account. There is tons of money available around the world, just waiting to be invested in a useful way, or to be grown. More money is available than investment opportunities. Do not limit yourself. It is not because this money is not currently available in your bank account. This could change. However, do not make the mistake to want to turn this $500 into to $5 million. Go ahead, systematically. Learn first to be a good trader. The money will follow eventually. Not the other way around.

Above all, you should first learn to appreciate what you have. If you have $500 to trade, then treat it as if that $500 was $500,000. Far too many starting traders do just the opposite. They are wasting the little they have. That little capital is not small. It is exactly the amount that you deserve right now. If you treat this sum in a responsibly way, then the universe will provide you soon with larger sums.

Leave it to the universe, how it proceeds. You know, it is infinite, and there are no limits.

I wish you success!

Heikin Ashi Trader

You can contact me here: pdevaere@yahoo.de

Glossary

Breakeven: The point at which gains equal losses.

Broker: A firm that charges a fee or commission for executing buy and sell orders submitted by an investor.

Compound Interest: Compound interest can be thought of as „interest on interest," and will make a deposit or a loan grow at a faster rate than simple interest, which is interest calculated only on the principal amount.

Day Trading: A trading strategy by which the trader closes out all trades before the market close and does not hold any open positions overnight.

Demo Account: A Demo Account is typically „funded" with simulated money, which allows the investor to conduct fictitious trades in order to become familiar with the ins and outs of the platform.

Drawdown: The maximum loss in value until reachievement of the original value.

Expectancy: The amount a trading system stand to gain, or lose, per dollar of risk.

Forex: The market in which currencies are traded.

Forex Pair: Two currencies with exchange rates that are traded in the forex market.

Leverage: The use of various financial instruments or borrowed capital to increase the potential return of an investment.

Lot: The standardized quantity of a financial instrument as set out by an exchange or similar regulatory body.

Managed accounts: A fee-based investment management product for high-net-worth inviduals.

Mini-Lot: A currency lot size that is 1/10 the size of the standard lot of 100,000 units.

Payoff Ratio: Average winning trade dollar amount divided by the average losing trade dollar amount.

Pip: The smallest price change that a given exchange rate can make.

Risk Management: A two-step process that determines what risks exist in an investment and then handling those risks in a way best-suited to the investor's investment objectives.

Scalping: A trading strategy that attempts to make many profits on small price changes.

Social Trading: The process through which online financial investors rely on user generated financial content.

Swing Trading: A style of trading that attempts to capture gains in a stock or a market within one to four days.

To go long: The buying of a security such as a stock, commodity or currency, with the expectation that the asset will rise in value.

To go short: The sale of a borrowed security, commodity or currency with the expectation that the asset will fall in value.

Track Record: The past performance of a trader viewed in its entirety.

Trailing Stop: A stop order that can be set at a defines percentage away from a security´s current market price.

Volatility: The amount of uncertainty or risk about the size of changes in a security's value.

More Books by Heikin Ashi Trader

How to Scalp the Mini DAX Futures?

Thanks to the introduction of the Mini-DAX futures (FDXM) private traders with smaller accounts are afforded the opportunity to scalp the German DAX Index to professional terms. Unlike most other trading instruments, Futures are the most transparent and effective way to make money in the financial markets.

Scalpers have infinitely more trading opportunities than position traders or day traders, which constitutes the real strength of this trading style. A scalper may therefore manage his capital much more effectively than all other market participants and thus achieve much greater returns than would otherwise be the case.

The Heikin Ashi Trader shows in this book how to successfully scalp this new future on the DAX. You will learn how to enter the market, how to manage your position and at which point you should back out. In addition, the book contains a wealth of tips and tools to make your trading even more effective and precise.

Table of Contents

1. The EUREX Introduces the Mini DAX Future

2. The German DAX, a Popular Market for International Traders

3. Advantages of Future Trading

4. The Heikin-Ashi Chart

5. What Is Scalping?

6. What is the Advantage of Being a Scalper?

7. Basic Setup of Heikin Ashi Scalping

8. Entry Strategies

9. Are Re-Entries Sensible?

10. Exit Strategies

11. Are Multiple Targets Sensible?

12. When You Should Scalp the Mini-DAX-Future (and When Not)

13. Useful Tools for Scalpers

A. Placing Orders

   B. Open and Close Orders

   C. Managing Open Orders

   D. The Trailing Stop as a Profit Maximization Tool

14. Various Stop-Orders

   A. The Fix Stop

   B. The Trailing Stop

   C. The Linear Stop

   D. The Time Stop

   E. The Parabolic Stop

   F. Link Stop Orders

   G. Multiple Stops and Multiple Targets

15. On the Stock Exchange Money Is Made with Exit Strategies!

16. Further Development of Market Analysis

   A. Key Price Levels

B. Live Statistics

Epilogue

Glossary

More Books by Heikin Ashi Trader

About the Author

About the Author

Heikin Ashi Trader is the pen name of a trader who has more than 15 years of experience in day trading futures and foreign exchange. He specializes in scalping and fast day trading. In addition to this, he has published multiple self-explanatory books on his trading activities. Popular topics are on: scalping, swing trading, money- and risk management.

Imprint

© 2017 Heikin Ashi Trader

The work including all contents is copyrighted. All rights reserved. No part of this publication may be reprinted or reproduced in any form or by any means, electronic, mechanical, photocopy or otherwise, without the express written permission of the author. All translation rights reserved.
The use of this book and the implementation of the information contained therein are expressly at your own risk. The work, including all content, has been compiled with utmost care. However, printing errors and misinformation cannot be completely excluded. The author accepts no liability for the topicality, correctness and completeness of the contents of the book, or for printing errors. There can be no legal responsibility as well as liability in any form for erroneous information and consequences resulting from the author. For the content of the Internet pages printed in this book, the operators of the respective internet pages are solely responsible.

First edition 2017

Text: © Copyright by HeikinAshi Trader
12 Carrer Italia, 5B
03003 Alicante, Spain
All rights reserved

Printed in Poland
by Amazon Fulfillment
Poland Sp. z o.o., Wrocław